SOLIDARITY NETWORKS & EMERGENCY SURVIVAL

CC-BY-NC-SA 2020 GODS&RADICALS PRESS
This work may be reproduced only for non-commercial reasons. All reproductions must bear attribution to the author and carry this identical license.

ISBN: 978-1-7325523-9-5

GODS&RADICALS PRESS

Layout by Gods&Radicals Press

For bulk, solidarity, and wholesale copies
please contact us at
distro@abeautifulresistance.com

See our other books and online journal at
ABEAUTIFULRESISTANCE.ORG

SOLIDARITY NETWORKS

Men brandishing assault rifles surround a building full of Black people. Groups of white men wearing biker's jackets bearing racist emblems roam the streets and make 'visits' to Mosques looking for signs of religious extremism. Nameless government soldiers kidnapping activists in unmarked vans. A right-wing media figure shows up to a protest, his pockets full of ammo rounds, and aims a gun at unarmed women and children. Refugees from economic collapse and brutal wars flood across borders, risking drowning or getting smashed by trains and trucks to sneak through tunnels or over oceans.

None of these events take place in an imaginary future. This is our present world, one where all the illusions of peace, prosperity, and 'civilization' are melting away. And it can get much worse. Probably will. We're watching an empire crumble, and it's not going down without a fight.

But before you despair, let me tell you what else has been happening.

Groups of people are smuggling fleeing refugees across borders. Some show up when gangs of white supremacists gather in city centers and fight them off. Thousands of people gather on sacred land to help indigenous people fight off government-approved explosive pipelines. People are risking imprisonment and death to fight police, the military, corporate security, and fascists to defend others. They're stockpiling birth control, teaching self-defense, and working to keep other people safe.

There are many names for these sorts of groups. They transcend race and nationality, religion and family and community, and even rarely fit squarely into usual political categories of left or right. And they seem to arise organically, always from the ground-up.

They're called Solidarity Networks, and they are crucial to our survival. They're also crucial for building a new world from the ruins of Capitalism and Empire.

You're probably already familiar with Solidarity Networks, though you might not realize it. Actually, you already have the beginnings of one, but we'll get to that in a bit.

During the 1800's in the United States of America, abolitionists, former slaves, First Nations people, and sympathetic allies maintained safe houses and transportation for Blacks attempting to flee slavery into British/Canadian territory. This was The Underground Railroad. They did so without a specific hierarchy, and not only without help from the government, but in direct opposition to it. It was illegal to shelter fugitive slaves, even in so-called 'free states.'

Another such network arose in Europe during the rise of the Nazi party and up to the end of World War II. Individuals and groups from many backgrounds and political persuasions sheltered, hid, and helped transport Jews and others out of Germany and Europe.

But helping fugitives is only one role of a solidarity network. In many cities in the United States, groups have been organized around helping immigrants and low-income folks get wages from cheating employers or deposits back from deadbeat landlords. Similarly non-hierarchical, their members aren't just 'activists': in fact, many involved are people who've been helped by the group before.

WHAT THEY ARE

Regardless of the specific purposes of any Solidarity Network, they share the following traits:

• They are intentional

While there are countless instances of people coming together to help others in need, a solidarity network isn't just a single spontaneous action. And though they often arise organically, they are held together by shared principles and commitments and require organization.

- **They are distributed, not authoritarian**

Solidarity networks have leaders and organizers, but the key to them is plurality. No one person is ever in charge of the network or the actions. Rather, the decisions are made by a group of people or, ideally, everyone involved. Not only does this prevent abuse, but it ensures that the network has more participation and can survive if something happens to core people.

- **They do not rely on government or the law**

Solidarity networks are never part of the government. In fact, they often arise in opposition to the government, or to fill a need that the government cannot fill (or has caused). For instance, both the Underground Railroad and the many people helping to hide Jews during World War II were engaged in illegal activities. Others use direct action to get justice where the laws have so many loopholes that official channels (such as the courts) always fail the poor.

- **They are political, but do not demand political conformity**

The Underground Railroad was heavily supported by abolitionists, many of whom were early socialists. However, just as many were not socialists. You did not have to be a socialist or abolitionist to help, nor did you need to conform to any religious belief. Likewise, Communists, Anarchists, Conservatives, and Liberals all worked together to get Jews out of Germany. While some political groups are much more likely to participate (and others likely to oppose the group), commitment to the cause is what is required, not identification with a party or political theory.

• They make the most vulnerable their priority

Solidarity networks don't help the oppressed as part of their work, *that is their work*. This makes them radically different from many other groups (like charities, churches, or unions) who come together for other purposes but include support for vulnerable people. Solidarity networks start from that support and center all their other activities around it.

WHAT THEY ARE NOT

As mentioned above, a solidarity network is different from other groups. It's important to keep these distinctions in mind.

• They are not communities

Community is a word used so often it doesn't really mean anything. We use it to describe both neighborhoods and identity-groups—like Pagan or LGBT 'communities'—as well as nebulous associations like the Online Gaming or Activist 'Community.' In all cases, community denotes a shared characteristic (living in the same neighborhood, playing online games) but not much else.

Solidarity networks are not based around identity, and do not rely on shared characteristics as a unifying principle.

• They are not institutions

This distinction is important. Charities, non-governmental organizations, non-profits, or other groups certainly do good work. Their downside is that they are top-heavy, slow, inefficient, and often rely on large groups of people donating money rather than time. Though a solidarity network might pool resources or ask for donations, direct action is more important.

• They are not political parties

Though every single member of a solidarity network might be politically engaged and be active in political parties, the network is not a party. Political parties seek to gain power through the electoral process, rather than direct action. This always leads to compromise of their founding goals and direct-action work.

• They are not advocacy groups

A solidarity network doesn't try to 'raise awareness' about the plight of the oppressed: it does something about it. While advocacy is often part of the work of a solidarity network, attempts to raise awareness are specifically used to bring more people within the network and to support their actions. Activism and advocacy are part of the actions, but are not the actions themselves.

CORE PRINCIPLES

No two networks are identical, nor should they be. But they do share several core principles, regardless of their differences.

- **Direct Action**

Solidarity Networks do not rely on the electoral, legal, or political process to enact change. The people who hid Jews in their apartments in Berlin understood the political process wouldn't help them, just as the former slaves and abolitionists who hid and transported fugitive Blacks did not wait to win court battles or get the right people in office.

Direct action means *action*. It means doing something tangible to help others, rather than giving passive and indirect support. It isn't a Facebook like or a Twitter re-tweet; it isn't holding a sign or writing to your senator. None of those things directly affect the situation of the oppressed. Likewise, direct action is *direct*. It does not rely on the powerful, on representatives or officials or leaders.

We have become very accustomed to passive support: calling 911 when someone is in distress, giving money to large organizations like The Red Cross or Amnesty International. We cannot always directly help those in need, but when we can, we must. And because we've become so passive, we will need to relearn what we are actually capable of.

• **Mutual Aid**

Mutual aid is a principle very much forgotten in capitalist countries, and it's one we need to remember immediately.

Mutual aid is based on the idea that every person within a solidarity network is as valuable as every other, and each much be supported equally. This is seen best in the following two statements.

"An injury to one is an injury to all."

Every act of violence, oppression, and harm that affects an individual also affects the group. Solidarity networks make a commitment to support each person and to come together in their defense.

This already occurs in solidarity networks designed to help workers and renters unfairly fired or evicted. Sometimes, those who became involved at the beginning to help others find themselves in the same situations as those they've helped. An activist might find themselves losing their job for unfair reasons and suddenly find people they helped helping them.

This principle is essential to the coherence of the group. Unlike communities formed around identity, everyone within a solidarity network commits to the well-being of everyone else. They are all allies, all accomplices, supporting each other whenever needed. Many oppressors isolate and target individuals: a group will always be much stronger.

"From each according to their ability, to each according to their need."

Solidarity networks also recognize that each person has different abilities, wealth, privilege, vulnerabilities, and needs. Therefore, though they treat each person as important as every other person, they acknowledge some can give more while some will need more.

This is best seen in the networks who supported fugitive Jews and Blacks. Escaped slaves had no property, often could not read or write, and often had nothing to offer. Similarly, fleeing Jews had few resources, no access to more, and often didn't speak the language of their hosts outside Germany. In these cases, to expect the Jews or Blacks to carry their own weight or pay for rent or for food would have been more than unfair.

That doesn't mean they were unable to give back. Many escaped slaves returned to help others along the Underground Railroad routes, many Jews helped watch the children of their hosts or offered financial help in return. But since a solidarity network prioritizes the most vulnerable, it will acknowledge that those they help probably cannot help back during their greatest needs.

RISK

Before we look at how we can build solidarity networks, we need to have an honest talk about risk.

We're not used to taking risks. In fact, if there's anything Liberal Democracy has been very good at, it is assuring us that it's always better to be safe, comfortable, and secure. Risk is for the foolish people, or for gamblers or stock market investors, not for everyday folk.

That's never been true for everyone. Life has never been safe, though if you're white, middle-class, able-bodied, straight, or otherwise privileged, you probably aren't accustomed to the idea that helping someone might throw you in jail or lead to your death. But many Black, trans, queer, poor, disabled, First Nations, immigrant, and many other people have known that the safety and security promised by capitalism and democracy has always been a lie. It's never been safe for them—even if they toe the line, even if they obey all the laws, even if they pay their rent on time and never drive above the speed limit.

Right now, it's mostly just middle class people who still cling to this illusion. Worse, the refusal of such people to take risks on behalf of others is one of the reasons why oppression has continued for so long.

As Liberal Democracy collapses around us, only some people will really have a choice to avoid risk. Stay silent, and you might be safe. Keep your head down, and you might not be targeted. Don't question oppression, and you might get to keep your jobs, your homes, and your normal life.

You might get to keep going as you did, while immigrants are rounded up and deported, more Blacks are murdered, vulnerable people die from lack of healthcare and medicine, trans people are beaten or kill themselves, First Nations people lose even more land and face down military-grade police forces...all for the chance that you might feel safe.

Do you really want that? You don't, because you're still reading.

Ready? Good.

STARTING A NETWORK

Every solidarity network is going to be different, and it'd be useless for us to give you a prescription for what you should do. Besides, it's time to give up our hope that leaders know any better than us and can get us out of this mess. You are the leader you've been waiting for.

Though we can't give you a prescription, we can outline a framework. Tinker with it at will, play with it, use your imagination. This is broad enough that you can adapt it any way you need to, but specific enough that you'll hopefully understand what's needed.

1. Start with your friends

We wrote earlier that you already have the beginnings of a solidarity network. They're called friends, and they're awesome.

Think about your closest friends. If you needed something right now, they'd be there for you, right? And if they needed something, you'd be there for them. Also, you don't always expect them to do the very same things that you do. They need different things, and can do different things.

Mutual aid and solidarity are not abstract principles. They're the foundation of friendship, and you're already really good at it. In fact, solidarity networks are radical friendships.

Also, you don't agree with everything your friends think, believe, or do. Maybe they vote differently, have different views on capitalism or religion or politics. But that doesn't stop your friendship, because friendship isn't based on those things. Neither are solidarity networks.

Think of a friend of yours who is as worried as you are about the way things are, hopefully someone who lives near you. Then, talk to them about what they need right now. They're probably pretty upset about the world right now and they could probably use a kind ear.

Ask them if they'd be willing to do something together to change stuff. Show them this essay if that helps. And then, together, talk about what you need from each other, what you can give to each other, and what you might be able to do together.

This may be an awkward conversation at first. Many people are not used to thinking of friendship this way. We take our friendships for granted, get lost in the passivity of internet communication and the weight of the world's sorrows. But if you want to build something better, this will be your first step.

Don't worry, though. This part is actually the easy part. They're your friends, after all.

2. Think about bodily and emotional needs

(DON'T SKIP THIS STEP!)

Another thing capitalism's been good at is distracting us from our bodies and emotions. We are often in our heads, thinking huge thoughts, worrying, fretting, plotting. So it's no surprise that so many people right now have been asking some very scary questions for the first time about how they'll survive all the chaos and violence as empire crumbles.

Ask the following questions of yourself first:

• What do you need to survive? Where does your food come from, your medicine, your shelter? How secure is all of that? What might happen if the way of getting that is disrupted?

• What do you need to feel safe? How many of the comforts in your life are only things that get you through the misery of your job? How much do you rely on police and the government for your bodily protection? What happens if that goes away?

• How do you deal with fear? Do you tend to shut down when crises happen, or do you put off emotions until the crisis is over? How do you manage panic, anxiety, depression, and despair? Do you rely on external sources (medications, entertainment, your friends and family) to get you through bad stuff, and what happens if they are not available in a crisis?

- What resources do you have? Do you have savings? A home, a car, other things that you might need if things get awful? Are you currently reliant on government income or benefits? What happens if those are taken away from you? Do you have any skills that don't pay the bills but could directly benefit someone in need.

- How do you care for yourself? Do you sometimes overextend your energy and resources? Are you good at communicating to people who support you when you need their help? Do you have trouble setting boundaries with people whom you support?

Once you've asked these questions of yourself, ask them of others. You don't necessarily need to directly ask them—you probably already know most of your friends' answers anyway. But to build a solidarity network, you need to understand not just your own abilities and needs, but those of others.

Thinking about your own situation and the precarious things that keep you safe will equip you to really understand the needs of others when they express them.

3. Extend out from your friends, and especially to people in need or danger

Solidarity networks are not communities. Communities are based on shared traits, while solidarity networks intentionally include oppressed people. Not only do they intentionally include them, they are built with them specifically in mind.

Here's the part where risk begins to come in. When you offer your support to someone in danger, you take on their danger. You share risk. Most friendships aren't based in unequal circumstances, but solidarity networks must be.

You don't need to go out looking for oppressed people. They are all around you. You are probably quite vulnerable yourself.

Right now, you know someone who needs you. Maybe you know them only from work or the bar or your neighborhood. They might be the illegal immigrant who cleans your office or washes dishes at the restaurant where you work. They might be your Black neighbor, or the Muslim clerk at the convenience store where you buy your cigarettes. They might be the friend you haven't heard from in years, who you know suffers from deep depression, or your co-worker who just started transitioning gender.

Ask them what you can do to support them. Dare an awkward conversation, and risk the possibility that they might rebuff you or be facing problems so big you might be overwhelmed. Your network can't help anyone if it doesn't risk reaching out.

4. Use Your Privilege

You need to understand your privilege, because that privilege might save someone's life.

If you're white, you should already know about your white privilege. If you don't, it's past time for you to learn. Middle class whites can walk by cops without getting shot, can walk into stores without getting followed. That's why many middle class whites don't take Black accounts of police oppression seriously–they don't experience it, and so have no reference point.

To build solidarity networks, you need to give that benefit to someone else. You can't change your privilege, but you can acknowledge that your privilege can be used to protect the life of a person who doesn't have that privilege:

- If you're white, you can get away with stuff your immigrant or Black friend can't.

- If you're male, you're safer at night than your female friends.

- If you are healthy and have no medical problems, you can do things your disabled friends cannot.

- Straight and cisgendered? Your body can be used to protect your gay and trans friends.

Really listen to the needs of those around you, recognize their vulnerabilities, and use your lack of them to help them. Use your white skin to protect a Black person from a cop, your male body to protect a woman from sexual assault, your able body to gather resources and do work a disabled person cannot.

"From each according to their ability…" doesn't just refer to money or skill. Your privilege gives you access to things other people don't get. Use it to get it for them.

5. Grow, spread, seed

Keep going. The more of you there are, the more you can do. The more you succeed, the more other people will be inspired to do the same thing. And the more experienced you get at this, the more you'll be able to teach others.

IMPORTANT CONCERNS

There are some other things to consider here.

Secrecy

If you're doing very risky illegal actions such as hiding immigrants or dissidents, you need what's called a 'security culture.' Every person involved in your network must commit to keeping your activities secret, must think beforehand what they will say if they are arrested, and must honestly consider how 'an injury to one' will apply if they're being tortured in prison.

If your group gets large and relies on lots of people who are more 'allies' than participants, consider the security culture of the Underground Railroad. People who ran safehouses rarely knew the location of many more of them, guides didn't always know each other, and slaves who were smuggled out didn't always even know the names of people who were helping them.

Such secrecy protected the entire network, and also helped get more people involved. If a fugitive slave, a guide, or a host was caught, no matter how much they were tortured, they could not reveal who was 'behind' the Underground Railroad. The entire network could survive because no one person knew all the secrets.

Beware of Authority

Your network is going to have organizers. More than likely, you'll be one of them if you started it. But there's a fine balance between being an organizer and being a central authority, and you must avoid the latter at all costs. This isn't just a matter of principle, though there are plenty of principled reasons to avoid top-down networks. It's a matter of survival for the entire group.

Police, military, mercenaries, and others will target the apparent leaders of a group. Being part of hierarchical, authoritarian groups themselves, they know how much chaos the loss of their own leaders would be. And if you have that kind of leader, the entire network can die when they are targeted.

As many people within the group as possible should share in the organizing role. That doesn't mean everyone needs to be an organizer, only that there needs to be several people able to fulfill the role at a moment's notice. Too much all on the shoulders of one organizer will crush that person anyway, leading to burnout, bitterness, and even the end of the network.

Prioritize Everyone's Needs—Including Yours

You can't save drowning people when you're drowning.

Every activist can tell you this, every organizer has a story. You'll be trying to help others, dedicating all your time and energy and resources, and then suddenly…you're done. You can't lift another finger, you can't be bothered to care. If it's bad enough, you actually start to resent or even hate the people you've been trying to help.

There are many reasons this happens, and it's a huge risk if you're one of the organizers of the network. If you have more 'ability' to begin with, you may forget your needs, especially if you're trying to keep up a strong mood of hope against a world of despair. When others are looking to you for help, it's really easy to ignore your own needs, especially if others aren't in a place to meet them.

The point of a solidarity network is that everyone is supported. Make sure you are too, whether that's setting stronger boundaries with people whose needs are too overwhelming for you at the moment or taking time away from organizing, especially before you start to shut down.

IDEAS

We've provided a very broad framework for solidarity networks, and used some specific examples to explain them. So you may be feeling a little overwhelmed. Are you capable of doing grand actions? Could you ever hope to be as courageous as others?

The examples provided were large for a reason. You are capable of all of that. You can save other people's lives, you can organize against bullies and the rich. And you may eventually have to.

But you don't have to start big. Here's a short list of places you might start.

• **Medication networks:** Many women, trans people, and medically-compromised folks may face a crisis over access to medications, birth control, and other necessary drugs. Do you have good health insurance? Don't need birth control but can get it? Access to pain, anxiety, or hormonal drugs that others might need? Build a network around this.

• **Emotional care networks**: Many, many minorities are terrified for their safety right now. Many are dealing with trauma and anxiety from what is happening and are feeling very isolated. Especially if you are worried but not yet directly affected by these crises, you can offer your emotional labor to them.

• **Skill, tool, transport, and resource share networks:** These are very common already. You know how to do things that others don't, skills that may be life-saving to others. Most people don't know how to sew, to cook food from scratch, to garden—skills once basic to humanity but long forgotten by many. Self-defense is another one that is very essential, especially for women, trans people, and people of color. Even something as common as owning a car means you have access to something many people don't have and might need. Building transport networks for people in dangerous areas can save lives.

- **Protection networks:** Never underestimate the value of being physically present for someone in danger. Are you an intimidating-looking male? Imagine if you and four others all show up to stand in front of a Black or immigrant-owned shop that's being targeted by racists. You don't have to be armed (though it might be a good idea); physical presence alone can often stop attacks.

There are countless other ways of doing this, and your network might evolve as you continue. A group dedicated to teaching people how to cook might also be an emotional care network, or later commit to drive immigrant women home from their night-cleaning jobs.

Whatever you commit to, the most important thing to do is start now. And as you do, know that others are doing the exact same thing. Some of those networks will connect to others, some will be official, others clandestine.

And one final note. We mentioned at the beginning that solidarity networks are a key to building the world we want. This is how we can prove to others and to ourselves that we don't need authority, we don't need corporations, we don't need government and police.

Not only are we standing up to violence and oppression, we're building a new world, one that we know is possible, because we're from there.

EMERGENCY SURVIVAL

Everything is just a bit much these days isn't it? I am reminded of a line from the Godspeed You! Black Emperor album *F#A#*. Between a couple of the songs is an interview taking place on the street:

"Do you believe the end of the world is coming?"

"The preacher man says it's the end of time. Says that America's rivers are going dry. The interest is up, the stock market is down. You guys got to be careful walking around here this late at night. This is the perfect place to get jumped."

"But do you think the end of the world is coming?"

"No, so says the preacher man, but I don't go by what he says."

That album was made back in 1997. 'The Dead Flag Blues' intro on that album is fantastic and listening to it today makes you wonder if they were prophets. Sure seems that the Empire of America is in its crumbling phase.

I also do not believe the preacher man. It is not yet time for the Apocalypse or Ragnarok or Kali Yuga. I do however see, with America in particular, a breakdown on the horizon. If you look at history and the collapse of other empires there are countless similarities to what America is going through.

But this is not a history lesson. Odds are, if you didn't already feel such things in your bones you wouldn't be reading this guide.

As someone who has spent the better part of the last 18 years working in emergency services, what I do is prepare to handle things when it all goes a bit pear shaped.

What I want to share with you is not any theories on what is going to happen, or how it will happen, or getting into step by step detail on how to survive specific scenarios. What this guide will go into is a return to basics and a simple theory on things to think about so you can care for yourself and your loved ones. When the structures of society that we are all quite used to either no longer exist, or are working against us, we need to be ready to care for ourselves.

Just in case the preacher man is right, yeah?

KNOWLEDGE, AWARENESS, & PREPARATION

We take a lot of things about our daily existence for granted. A good practice is to ask yourself questions you do not normally ask so you will be prepared in emergencies.

Here's an example. Let's say there is a protest march scheduled for today. Find out what the route is and the time. Will it affect the bus route you take home from work? What if you can't take the bus home? How far is the walk? What time do you get off work? If a curfew gets put in place could you walk home before a curfew would get put in place? What would you eat and drink along the way?

Food and transportation are two things we do not usually think about. I don't know about you, but when I got done with work I usually was hungry and ready for food. If I had to walk 5 miles home, perhaps uphill, and didn't have money or access to food, it wouldn't kill me but it would definitely suck. So maybe start keeping a couple granola bars in your work bag along with a bottle of water. Do you check the weather when you leave for work? When you dress, is it based on the fact that you will be warm and dry in your car? What happens if you can't drive home and have to walk in winter weather?

Another lesson of survival is thinking laterally. Ask yourself questions, but don't stop when you have come up with a solution to a problem with the first step. Think two or three steps down the line.

Also think about likelihood vs impact. This is how governments determine how much effort and resources to devote to preparedness. Zombies, for example, would have high impact but low likelihood, so they do not prepare for them.

Winter weather tends to be in the middle of this scale (and is affected by location—think New York City vs. Seattle).

The best way for you and the people around you to survive any major event is to come together to help each other out. Is one of your neighbors a medic that could help out with medical care? Does one of your neighbors have a garden where they grow vegetables? Does one do a lot of camping and have tents and sleeping bags?

Yes, we all have immediate survival needs which I will touch on, but while we may have enough food and water to live, we need community support.

THE BASICS

If you believe the US Army, they go by the rule of threes. 3 minutes without oxygen, 3 hours in extreme weather without shelter, 3 days without water, and 3 weeks without food.

Guess what? The military is quite good at survival manuals. Why? Well, at the end of the day, even an infantryman is expensive to train, an Air

Force pilot even more so. The Air Force survival manual is the most detailed survival manual I have ever come across. The military is quite good at trying to kill others, but at the end of the day it wants its own soldiers to stay alive.

So why is the rule of the 3's important? It is the basis for survival. Those are the things that will kill you. If you can sort those out, you will have time to figure everything else out.

To bring this into your day-to-day life, let's look at food and water. How would you eat dinner tonight if you could not go to the shop or have a functioning stove? Think about breakfast tomorrow, then lunch, then dinner again. What about water to cook that food with, or clean with after? How would you wash your dishes or brush your teeth?

When it comes to taking care of one's self, sort out the basics. This will give you a foundation that will help you keep your head clear when things go bad. One thing that came out of the earthquake in Japan in 2011 is that quite a lot of people were used to daily trips to the shops for food or even did not cook for themselves and ate out all the time. When power was down and shops and restaurants closed, people had no stockpiled food and some didn't know how to cook. These days there are services that deliver prepped meals to your door, microwave quick meals are available at supermarkets, but how available will these be for you if there is no power?

I experienced a similar thing as a kid in Seattle where one Christmas close to a foot of snow was dumped over a couple days, including Christmas Day. Power was out at the local grocery store, food deliveries were delayed due to road issues, but because my family had a general habit of keeping a good stock of staples, we did not go hungry.

WHAT ARE YOUR NEEDS?

If you want to prepare yourself divide your needs into three categories: Red, Yellow, and Green.

Red: Without these things, nothing else will be possible.

Reds are what will keep you alive. Use the rule of threes as a basis for your plan. Remember to think about particulars to your personal situation. If you have a backyard you may be able to cook on an open fire; if you have an apartment with a deck you could use a small grill. But if you have neither, using a grill inside is a good way to kill yourself because of inadequate ventilation. Natural gas camp-style stoves are safe in a room because there is minimal off-gassing, but long term burning can be dangerous in a small room so don't use it for heat.

You can purchase (online or at surplus stores) military MREs (Meals Ready to Eat) and some of these come with their own heating packets. These allow you to heat the meal without an external source. Plenty of calories and the full meal kits usually come with a tasty treat like M&M's! They also last forever. My own practice was to have 14 in my truck and 14 in my apartment. This would keep me alive for 28 days without any other source of food, or allow me to share with others. The reason I split them up was in case I was at work when things went bad or my apartment collapsed due to an earthquake, I would still have half my food supply.

Maybe you live near a stream that flows year round. Could you perhaps buy a camping-style water purifier or water-purification tablets instead of stockpiling bottles of water? A person needs a gallon of water per day, half for drinking, half for cooking and hygiene. Remember to think laterally, though. What happens if you have a friend in town staying with you when stuff happens? Would you really deny a neighbor who asks for help?

Another thing to add to this list is medication. If you take medications on a daily basis, make sure to not let your prescriptions get low. This is particularly important for medications taken for mental health reasons or other chronic health issues. The side effects of being off them can be life threatening in and of themselves, especially without access to any sort of support networks.

Again, think laterally. It is all well and good to have supplies in your house. but you may not be home when things go bad. For most of us, unfortunately, we spend most of our time outside of the house at our place of work. How would you survive if something happened while you were at work? Could you walk home? An average able-bodied person walks at 3-4 miles per hour over level ground. If you can't walk home, do you have friends that live nearby? Could you store some supplies and just shelter for a while at work? Perhaps a possibility if you work in an office, not so much if you are a waitress at a restaurant. But good news if you work at a restaurant: you have ready access to food! Same for you grocery store workers out there.

Later, I will touch on putting together a "bug out" bag. This is a backpack that you keep that has the basics for survival that you always keep in one bag and keep accessible whenever possible. I used to keep mine in my truck so that whether I was home, at work, or visiting friends, it was there.

Yellow: I'm not dying, but I've got stuff to do.

These are the things that are helpful but not necessary for immediate survival. One example would be a pair of heavy duty work gloves. These are great for clearing debris or throwing tear gas canisters back at the police.

Also rope. As Samwise Gamgee said, "Rope! You'll want it, if you haven't got it!" A good length of 50 foot rope can be picked up at boating shops in particular. It doesn't have to be climbing style as that is quite expensive and you most likely will not be needing it to haul an adult up the side of a cliff. It can be more used for building shelters and the like. Also picking up some smaller parachute cord from a surplus store is quite handy and very inexpensive.

Tarps are also great to keep around. A tarp, a tree, and some parachute cord are all you need for a shelter that will keep you relatively warm and dry in most weather conditions.

Another thing to consider is: Do you know how to turn off the gas, water, and electricity mains to the place where you live? This is important for a variety of reasons. The main one is for those of you in earthquake or hurricane areas where you face the risk of building collapse. More people tend to die due to fires caused by gas leaks post-earthquake than from the actual quake itself. Being able to turn off your water can be important if the water supply becomes compromised. You can turn off the mains to the house and use what is already stored in the boiler.

Green: What's the point of living if I don't have tea?

There are plenty of examples of people having plenty of supplies and still dying. There are also plenty of examples of those with no supplies managing to stay alive. It often boils down to mental strength and morale, and that's what this category is.

Green items are those that make life worth living. But please don't buy a mini solar panel from REI with a USB port just so you can keep playing candycrush on your iPhone. There will be more exciting things to do after the collapse!

In all seriousness, think about something that will bring a bit of happiness to your life. Tea, a can of soda, chocolate, a deck of cards, a favorite book, a journal, colored pencils and paper... These are all small, relatively light things that can be that bit of happiness while the world is falling apart around you.

COMMUNITY

Our culture loves the idea of the lone wanderer in the apocalypse, from Mel Gibson in 'Mad Max', to Denzel Washington in 'Book of Eli', to Robinson Crusoe, to the Fallout series of video games. Realistically, it is much harder and less likely that anyone can survive without community.

After the collapse of the Roman Empire in Europe, communities still survived by working together. There was really no need for a central government. That is why the fear of the collapse of civilization is somewhat silly to me. First off, what does civilization mean anyways? Seems an unnecessary construct that was created to impose a belief system on others and make it seem like a central government is necessary. Historically speaking, we as humans do pretty well on our own without being civilized.

But I digress. Working together is the key to getting beyond the survival mode and into the living mode. So think about your community. There are many definitions for this; it could be the social group you are a part of, more so than the other people in your apartment building. Either way, start talking to them now and think about what you are each good at or want to learn about to help each other. Maybe none of you has any medical training, so one of you takes a first aid course. Money is tight for all of us, so pool resources. Each person could perhaps contribute to buying heirloom seeds. One person can take the time to research what edible foods can be planted in your area, and another person take some basic carpentry classes.

Another thing I can recommend is taking courses. One really good government resource is the CERT (community emergency response teams) program put on by FEMA. This program is built around the theory that emergency services provisions will not be available for the first 48-72 hours following a massive incident. I have done some teaching for this program, and what is most beneficial is that it gives you hands-on experience in dealing with various issues. How many of you have actually used a fire extinguisher on a fire? You get to do that on this course.

These are all volunteer, non-governmental people that take these courses. Usually it is a community group, or people from the same cul-de-sac or village that get together to take the course together. Not only does it provide practical knowledge and hands-on experience but it gives a group a chance to work and learn together. The website for info is on the main FEMA page—get it while it's still available.

VIOLENCE AND SELF-DEFENCE

I want to touch briefly on the more violent side of things.

As the old saying goes, the best way to survive a knife fight is to not get into one in the first place. How is the best way to avoid this? Situational awareness. Vigilance. Being aware of your surroundings and knowledge of de-escalation. Just basic street smarts, but these days so many people get so used to walking with ear buds in and staring at their iPhones. If wolves still roamed the streets, they would have a feast.

That being said, sometimes you have to throw down. Like everything I have written about so far, knowledge and preparation will mean the difference between life and death. Take a self-defense class. Lift heavy things to build strength. If you decide to purchase a weapon, even something like pepper spray, practice with it. Just make sure you know the wind direction so you don't spray yourself in the face.

I am not going to sit here and preach to you on the goodness or badness of violence. Statistically speaking, most people will never actually be in a violent situation. Unfortunately, the odds go up significantly if you belong to a non-white-male group, because you will get targeted by the majority white male group.

All I can say in this brief document is that if you find yourself in a scrap, you have to act without hesitation, without holding back. Be decisive in your actions. Once you start don't stop until you and those you are protecting are safe. I say this from many violent encounters from years in the ambulance service. People having a mental health crisis who truly believe you are the devil trying to steal their soul can become very violent and very forceful. I became quite good at knowing where that line was, and knew that once that situation crossed that line I would either have to remove myself completely to a place of safety, or get stuck in and hope I could hold my own until the police arrived. In this new environment, I suspect the police are not the people that will be coming to help you.

That leads me into the next bit, again about community and helping each other out. If you see a violent confrontation developing, a lot of times numbers can cause an aggressive group to turn away. Particularly if it's a group of frat boys deciding to corner an individual, the more people that arrive to stand with them, the more likely they'll back off.

So what should you do after reading this? Have a tea party. Invite those that you feel connections to over and talk. Get pieces of paper and write Red, Yellow, Green at the top and start thinking about the things you need. Learn about each other, who is good at what, who has a friend who knows how to do a thing and can teach everyone. Consider building a Solidarity Network. Remember: You all are in this together. Go carefully and be the shield wall against the darkness.

THE "OH, SHIT!" BAG

Here's what my own emergency supplies look like. Adjust according to your own circumstances.

72-hour bag:

- Sleeping bag (30-degree) in waterproof stuff sack
- Footprint from ½ dome tent
- Tarp (One side brown, other green)
- 50 feet of rope
- Flat water pack
- Assorted maps of local wilderness
- Plastic map case
- Passport
- 1 novel (morale item)
- 1 deck cards (morale item)
- 1 notebook
- 3 assorted clippable black pouches
- Mug
- Work gloves
- Camp towel
- Waterproof cover for pack
- Olive drab medic shoulder bag

Clothes:
- Rain jacket
- Fleece
- Long underwear, top and bottom
- 2 pairs wool socks
- 1 pair white cotton underwear
- 1 pair boxers
- 1 fleece cap
- 1 black cargo trousers
- 1 long-sleeve athletic shirt

Food:
- 8 granola bars
- 5 packs fruit snacks
- 5 vitamin drink packs
- 1 Pack jerky
- 1 Pack tuna
- Small bag trail mix

Survival Pack (attached to outside of pack)
- Parachute cord
- Trauma shears

- Small light
- Clear goggles
- Sunglass goggles
- Large Swiss Army Knife
- Compass
- Hand sanitizer
- 7 tent stakes

Fire kit (in survival pack):
- Flint spark
- Lighter
- Matches
- White fire starter

First Aid Kit:
- Emergency blanket
- 4-inch roller gauze
- 2 tongue depressors
- Wilderness first-aid guide
- 1-inch clear tape
- 5 x 9 Combi pad
- 1 sterile occlusive dressing

- 1 4 x 4 burn gel dressing
- Assorted small burn gel packs
- Multiple triple antibiotic packs
- 5 self-adhearing bandages
- Various alcohol prep pads
- 2 pairs gloves
- Pack of ibuprofen
- Pen and small pad

GODS&RADICALS PRESS

Gods&Radicals Press is a not-for-profit Pagan anti-capitalist publisher.

For more of our works or to order bulk copies of this book, please contact us at:

Distro@ABeautifulResistance.com

or visit our website at:

ABEAUTIFULRESISTANCE.ORG

www.ingramcontent.com/pod-product-compliance
Lightning Source LLC
Chambersburg PA
CBHW071322080526
44587CB00018B/3326